Molly Brown

Molly Brown

Community BUILDERS

Sharing Her Good Fortune

by
Charnan
Simon

Children's Press®
A Division of Grolier Publishing
New York / London / Hong Kong / Sydney
Danbury, Connecticut

Photo Credits

Photographs ©: AP/Wide World Photos: 8 (Horace Cort), 31 (Bob Daugherty), 32 (Wilson), 15, 16, 18, 25 center, 28, 29, 34; Archive Photos: 38 (Corinne Dufka/Reuters), back cover (Steve Jaffe/Reuters), 2 (Mike Theiler/Reuters), 12, 17, 19, 24, 26; Corbis-Bettmann: 6, 9 (AFP), 40 (Robert Maass), 25 top (Wally McNamee), 3 (Joseph Sohm/ChromoSohm, Inc.), 10, 23, 35 (UPI), 25 bottom; Jimmy Carter National Historic Site: 13; Liaison Agency, Inc.: cover (William Coupon), 43 (Gifford); NDI/Carter Center: 37 (Yuriah Tanzil); PhotoEdit: 44 (Tony Freeman); Sygma: 20 (Arthur Grace).

Visit Children's Press on the Internet at:
http://publishing.grolier.com

Library of Congress Cataloging-in-Publication Data

Simon, Charnan
    Molly Brown : sharing her good fortune / by Charnan Simon.
        p. cm. — (Community builders)
    Includes bibliographical references and index.
    Summary: Relates the life story of Molly Brown, who rose from humble beginnings to great wealth through the Colorado Gold Rush, survived the Titanic, and was active in social reform.
    ISBN: 0-516-21606-6
    1. Brown, Margaret Tobin, 1867-1932—Juvenile literature. 2. Colorado—Biography—Juvenile literature. [1. Brown, Margaret Tobin, 1867–1932. 2. Colorado—Biography.] I. Title. II. Series.
CT275.B7656 S56 2000
978.8'03'092—dc21
[B]   99-087477

Contents

**Molly Brown in Newport, Rhode Island,
years after the *Titanic* disaster**

Chapter ONE

The Legend of Molly Brown

Molly Brown was a real, live woman—and a legend in her own lifetime. Bold, generous, and outspoken, she lived a life of action and adventure at a time when most women were content to stay quietly at home.

One of Molly Brown's most dramatic adventures occurred in 1912. Molly was a passenger on the *Titanic* when the ship struck an iceberg and sank in the Atlantic Ocean. Surviving the *Titanic* disaster earned her the nickname of "unsinkable" Molly Brown.

Molly Brown was famous even before her *Titanic* adventure. She was born poor, but became rich

The *Titanic*

The Titanic was a British ocean liner—a cruise ship. When it was built, the *Titanic* was the largest ship in the world. All the experts said it was unsinkable. But on April 14, 1912, during the *Titanic's* very first voyage from England to New York City, the ship hit an iceberg and sank. More than 1,500 people were drowned in the tragedy. Only 700 people, mostly women and children, were saved in the *Titanic's* lifeboats.

A scene of the *Titanic* sinking from the movie *Titanic*

Margaret was Molly Brown's real first name.

because of the success of Colorado gold mines. She spent her life—and her money—exploring the world and helping others. Because she was one of the most interesting and adventurous women of her day, stories sprang up about her while she was still alive. One story said that as the *Titanic* sank, Molly entertained her fellow lifeboat survivors by yodeling and doing gun tricks. According to another tale, Molly was born during a tornado and raised by a nanny goat. Some people said she paved the floors in her house with silver dollars!

Molly or Margaret?

Since Margaret Tobin Brown's death in 1932, she has been called "Molly Brown" in newspapers, magazines, books, radio shows, plays, and movies. Two of the most famous movies to call her "Molly" are *The Unsinkable Molly Brown*, which was made in 1964, and *Titanic*, made in 1997. Many people know Margaret Brown only as "Molly." But because

The stories continued and the legend grew after Molly Brown died. She became the subject of books, a musical play, and even a Hollywood movie. The stories about Molly were all very entertaining, but they just didn't tell the truth about her life. They didn't even use her true name! The woman we call "Molly Brown" was really named Margaret Tobin Brown. When she was a child, her family called her

this is a true book about a real person, "Molly" will be called by her real name— Margaret Tobin Brown.

Actress Kathy Bates playing Molly Brown in the 1997 movie *Titanic*

Maggie. But no one ever called her Molly—until she became a character in a play and a movie!

Margaret Brown didn't need people to make up stories about her life. Her real adventures were exciting enough. She traveled the world, learned new languages, met famous people, stood up for what she believed in—and always found ways to share her good fortune with others.

Chapter TWO

Growing Up in Hannibal

On July 18, 1867, in the Mississippi River town of Hannibal, Missouri, John and Johanna Tobin had a baby daughter named Margaret. Her parents decided to call her Maggie for short.

Maggie was a happy, healthy little girl. She grew up surrounded by a loving Irish-Catholic family. Besides her parents, there were two older half-sisters, an older brother, and a younger brother and sister. When Maggie was old enough to start school, she walked down the street to her Aunt Mary O'Leary's house. Aunt Mary taught classes for most of the neighborhood boys and girls.

12

Hannibal, Missouri, and Mark Twain

Mark Twain

The small town of Hannibal lies along the Mississippi River in the northeastern part of Missouri. When Maggie was growing up, Hannibal was home to nearly 7,000 citizens. Today, some 18,000 people live there. Hannibal is famous for being the boyhood home of the writer Mark Twain (whose real name was Samuel Clemens). Mark Twain, who lived from 1835 to 1910, was one of America's greatest writers. When young Twain was growing up in Hannibal, he was fascinated by the colorful steamboats traveling up and down the busy Mississippi. Many of his books, such as *The Adventures of Tom Sawyer* and *Adventures of Huckleberry Finn,* include rich detail about life along the Mississippi.

**The house where Margaret was born
in Hannibal, Missouri**

Maggie's parents firmly believed that every child deserved an education. They also believed that all people deserved to be treated fairly, no matter what their color or background. In the years when Maggie grew up just after the Civil War, many people did not agree with John and Johanna Tobin. But Maggie's parents did not care what other people thought. They taught Maggie to follow her conscience and do what she thought was right.

14

The Civil War

The Civil War was fought by the Southern and Northern states from 1861 to 1865. The Southern states were fighting for their way of life, which included slavery. The Northern states were fighting to stop slavery and keep the country together. More than 600,000 soldiers died in the Civil War, more than in any other war in the history of the United States. Maggie Tobin's home state of Missouri was caught between the North and the South during the Civil War. Some 40,000 Missouri men fought for the South in the Confederate army during the war. Another 110,000 Missouri men fought for the North in the Union army.

Throughout her life, Margaret looked after her family.

When she was thirteen, Maggie left school. Like many other Hannibal girls of her age, Maggie went to work for the huge Garth Tobacco Factory. Stripping tobacco leaves from their prickly stems was hard work, and it didn't pay well. But Maggie was determined to help support her family. It hurt her to see how hard her father struggled to earn a living. "I longed to be rich enough to give him a home so that he would not have to work," she later said.

It wasn't long before Maggie had a chance to follow her dream. Her half-sister Mary Ann headed west to the newly discovered Colorado silver mines with her husband Jack Landrigan in 1883. Daniel followed in 1885, and by the spring of 1886, Maggie—now called Margaret—was ready to follow. The mines were flourishing in a town called Leadville, and nineteen-year-old Margaret Tobin wanted to be part of the action.

16

The Greatest Mining Camp in the World

Leadville, Colorado, is perched 10,000 feet (3,048 meters) high in the Mosquito Range. The town was founded in 1859, when gold was discovered in its rocky hills. But the gold soon dwindled, and it wasn't until 1870 that miners discovered the silver that would make Leadville famous. By 1880, Leadville, known as "the greatest mining camp in the world," had blossomed into Colorado's second-largest city.

Leadville, Colorado

Margaret Tobin may have stayed with her half-sister and brother-in-law when she first arrived in Leadville, but she soon moved in with her brother Daniel. She took care of the house while Daniel worked. Housekeeping wasn't enough for energetic, ambitious Margaret, however. She soon found a job sewing carpets and curtains in Leadville's largest

Who Lived in Leadville?

The early settlers in Leadville came from all over the world. They included silver and copper miners from Mexico and tin miners from England, as well as Danes, Norwegians, Swedes, and Irish. The Chinese, who had helped build the railroads that shipped the ore back East, were considered outcasts. So were the Utes—the Native American people who had originally lived in the area. As the city grew, immigrants from southern and eastern Europe were attracted by the plentiful opportunities for work in the mines.

dry goods store. The hours were long and the pay was poor, but Margaret was determined to pay her share of the bills.

Margaret hadn't forgotten her dream of becoming rich enough to take care of her family. Part of her plan included marrying a rich man, but these plans changed when she met a thirty-one-year-old Irishman named James Joseph Brown.

Known as J. J., or Jim, Brown was tall and handsome, ambitious and energetic. He had a steady job as a silver mine superintendent, but he was far from rich. In fact, he was almost as poor as Margaret herself. The two young people were instantly attracted to each other though, and soon fell in love. On September 1, 1886, she and J. J. were married.

Years later, Margaret told a newspaper interviewer about her courtship with J. J. Brown. "I wanted a rich man, but I loved Jim Brown. Jim was as poor as we were, and had no better chance in life. I struggled hard with myself in those days. Finally I decided that I'd be better off with a poor man whom I loved than with a wealthy one whose money had attracted me. So I married Jim Brown. I gave up cooking for my brother and moved to Jim's cabin, where the work was just as hard."

20

Margaret with her son Lawrence and her sister Ellen Tobin

Life was certainly not easy in J. J.'s two-room cabin on Iron Hill, but the newly-weds were happy. While J. J. steadily worked his way up in the silver mine business, Margaret took care of the house. She also found time to continue her education. Although she stopped going to school when she was thirteen, Margaret never stopped learning. Right after she was married, she hired a tutor to teach her about literature. Another teacher guided her in music, piano, and singing.

Margaret and J. J.'s first child, Lawrence Palmer Brown, was born on August 30, 1887. Then, on July 1, 1889, their daughter Catherine Ellen (called Helen after Margaret's favorite sister) was born. With their growing family, Margaret and J. J. moved to a bigger house in Leadville.

J. J. was doing very well in his job. He and Margaret weren't rich yet, but they were getting there. They began to take their

Helen, J. J., Margaret, and Lawrence Brown

place among Leadville's leading citizens.

Margaret was soon volunteering her time and energy for a variety of good causes. Even though J. J. was one of the "bosses," she sympathized with the miners and organized soup kitchens to help feed their families. She worked for better schools and better health care. She was also active in local and

Mining Operations

By the 1880s, mining was a big business. It was no longer possible for a single miner to "strike it rich" all by himself. Large corporations were formed to pay for the machines and manpower needed to reach rich silver deposits deep inside the mountains. For the owners, engineers, and superintendents, mining could be very profitable. For the thousands of workers who labored underground ten to twelve hours a day, mining was dangerous and low-paying work.

state politics. Leadville's citizens recognized Margaret by her beautiful team of matched black horses, her fancy hats, and the makeup she wore—when "face paint" was still considered "shocking."

Striking It Rich

In 1893, Margaret and J. J. got the break they were waiting for. J. J. had become mining superintendent for all the properties of the Ibex Mining Company, and gold was discoverd in one of J. J's mines. The mine—Little Jonny—was soon shipping more than 135 tons of gold ore a day. J. J. was given 12,500 shares of stock and named a member of the Ibex board of directors as a reward for his hard work. By the end of that year, J. J. and Margaret Brown were millionaires.

Margaret and J. J. celebrated by taking their family on a trip around the United States for sev-

The Little Jonny Mine

eral months. When they returned to Colorado, they decided to leave Leadville and settle in Denver.

Margaret was busier than ever in Denver. Besides their home on Pennsylvania Avenue (now Pennsylvania Street), she and J. J. built a ranch named Avoca about 9 miles (14.5 km) out of town.

Denver

Denver is the capital city of Colorado and an important manufacturing and transportation center for the Rocky Mountain states. It was founded by gold prospectors in 1858, and today it is home to nearly half a million people. In Margaret Brown's time, Denver was known as the Queen City of the Plains. Its citizens compared it proudly to other major American cities, such as Chicago and New York. Today, Denver is sometimes called the Mile High City, because the Capitol stands on land 1 mile (1.6 kilometers) above sea level.

Outside and inside of Margaret's home in Denver

For the next ten years, they would spend winters in their town house and summers at their lovely country retreat.

While J. J. worked harder than ever on his mines, Margaret threw herself into the social and political life of Denver. She became one of the founding members of the Denver Women's Club. With other club members, she helped organize traveling library and art exhibits for schools. She started community vegetable gardens to feed Denver's less fortunate

**Margaret in one
of her fancy dresses**

citizens. She also set up public health clinics for miners, immigrants, and others who couldn't afford to pay for medical care.

Margaret did more. She personally organized monthly entertainment at Denver's Working Girls' Home and the Young Women's Christian Association. Through the River Front Park project, she raised funds for a playground and summer school for 500 of Denver's neediest children.

One of Margaret's closest friends in Denver was Judge Benjamin Lindsey. Lindsey, a pioneer for the rights of children, almost single-handedly reformed the juvenile justice system in the United States. Margaret took an instant liking to

**Judge Benjamin
Lindsey**

Women's Clubs

In the late 1800s and early 1900s, most women were denied opportunities that men took for granted. Women were not allowed to vote or run for public office, and they couldn't work in most jobs. Many women turned to club work as a way to use their talents and energies to help their communities. Women's clubs raised money for good causes, supported education and the arts, and worked for political change.

Lindsey and tirelessly supported his efforts to improve the lives of Denver's children. She began a series of annual benefits to raise money for the Juvenile Aid Society. She helped build day nurseries, public playgrounds, and juvenile detention homes. She spoke out in favor of Lindsey's reform efforts, which eventually led to America's first juvenile court.

One of the social events that the Browns attended in Denver

Some of the more "proper" Denver society ladies were taken aback by Margaret's brash, outspoken, and energetic style. But no one could deny that she knew how to get things done. As a newspaper article of the time wrote about one of Margaret's many fund-raisers, "With Mrs. J. J. Brown's indomitable pluck and energy at its head, it is certain to be a great social and financial success."

Margaret and J. J. had time for fun, too. They both loved theater and opera, and the newspapers regularly wrote about the luncheons, teas, dinners, and other social events hosted by the Browns.

Margaret also discovered that she loved traveling and had a flair for learning languages. She began taking regular trips to Europe, Asia, and Africa. Sometimes she traveled with J. J. and the children. Sometimes she went with friends and sometimes she traveled alone. Wherever she went, Margaret learned all she could about the cultures and the people she met.

Margaret used her knowledge of other countries when she hosted her biggest fund-raiser ever—the

The dedication of the new Catholic cathedral in 1912

1906 Carnival of Nations. Margaret created a series of "living history" villages representing cultures from around the world, like a miniature World's Fair, to raise money for a new Catholic cathedral in Denver.

Margaret was busier than ever at home, too. In 1903, her sister-in-law Mary died, leaving Daniel Tobin with four young children between the ages of five and eleven. Without a moment's hesitation, Margaret took her three nieces into her home to be raised right along with Lawrence and Helen. Her nephew lived with other relatives, but visited often.

Margaret's three nieces, Grace, Helen, and Florence Tobin, in 1914

By now Margaret was rich enough to take care of her mother and father. In fact, most of the Tobin side of the family had followed Margaret to Denver. J. J. hired many of Margaret's relatives to work in his mines. J. J. and Margaret were both happy to be able to help their loved ones in any way they could.

J. J. Brown

There was only one dark cloud on Margaret's horizon. As the years went on, J. J. was always busy with his mines and business traveling. Margaret was always busy with her social and political causes, and with her own traveling. The two were growing further and further apart. Finally, J. J. and Margaret became legally separated in 1909. They never divorced, but were still separated when J. J. died in 1922.

Margaret and her daughter Helen in Egypt

Chapter FIVE

The Unsinkable Margaret Brown

In April 1912, Margaret Brown was in the middle of a wonderful overseas vacation with her daughter Helen. They had enjoyed riding camels in Egypt and visited historic sites in Italy, France, and England. But Margaret cut her trip short when she received a telegram from her son Lawrence. Married and the proud father of a baby boy, Lawrence sent his mother the bad news that her grandson, little Lawrence, Jr., was gravely ill.

The Titanic days before the disaster

Margaret immediately booked a passage on the next ship headed to the United States—the mighty *Titanic*. The *Titanic* had been at sea for only four days when it hit an iceberg in the middle of the night. The ship sank within hours about 400 miles (640 km) southeast of Newfoundland.

Margaret was one of the lucky ones. She made it into a lifeboat on that cold, dark night and quickly took charge. She handed out her own warm clothing to the freezing women and children in the lifeboat with her. She made sure everyone kept rowing to keep their blood circulating and to help them stay alive. And when the people in the lifeboat were finally rescued by another ship, the *Carpathia,* Margaret went right on helping her fellow survivors.

As a first-class passenger, Margaret Brown could have simply retired to a comfortable room on the *Carpathia.* Instead, she worked tirelessly to help the less fortunate second- and third-class passengers from the *Titanic.* She found food, blankets, and warm drinks for frightened children and women, many of whom spoke no English. Margaret's talent for languages

Margaret escaped from the sinking ship on a lifeboat like this one.

was put to good use as she explained, comforted, and translated for immigrants who had lost everything—family and friends, clothes, money, and valuables.

First-, Second-, or Third-Class?

It took nearly a week to cross the Atlantic Ocean in a large ship like the *Titanic*. First-class passengers like Margaret Brown paid a great deal of money for the luxury of a stateroom on the long voyage in the ocean liner. Second-class passengers had smaller—but still comfortable—rooms. Third-class passengers were crowded on the lower decks in very cramped and uncomfortable rooms.

Margaret did more. She and other wealthy women took up a collection from the rich first-class passengers on behalf of "the poor foreigners who, with everything lost, would be friendless in a strange country." When the *Carpathia* reached New York, Margaret refused to rest until she was certain her new immigrant friends had found the proper care and shelter.

Newspapers around the country hailed "the unsinkable Mrs. Brown." For the rest of her life, Margaret would be famous for her heroism during the *Titanic*'s sinking. Pleased that newspapers

Margaret presents Captain Rostron of *Carpathia* with a silver cup.

everywhere would now write about her activities, she continued to speak out about causes that were important to her.

Margaret used her fame to good purpose. She made speeches in favor of shorter working hours for factory workers, minimum wages for women, and women's right to vote. She spoke out for affordable child care, education reform, and a better justice system. She even ran for a seat in Congress in 1914, but later withdrew from the race.

Margaret, on the far left, at social event in France

Margaret also continued to travel widely, and especially loved spending time in France. During World War I (1914-1918), she devoted herself to Red Cross work in France, and to helping rebuild parts of the country that were destroyed by the fighting. Her efforts were rewarded in April 1932, when she was awarded France's highest award—the French Legion of Honor.

Margaret in 1927

Margaret's last years were spent traveling, lecturing, and satisfying her lifelong dream of learning to act. Wherever she was and whatever she was doing, she never forgot the Colorado miners who had been so much a part of her early life. Every Christmas, she sent a huge shipment of clothing,

41

candy, and hundreds of pairs of children's socks to Leadville's neediest families.

Margaret Brown died suddenly on October 26, 1932, in New York City. She once described herself as "a daughter of adventure," and that was certainly the way she tried to live her life. And though her earliest ambition had been merely to be rich, that ambition changed over the years. Shortly after her *Titanic* adventure, Margaret told a newspaper reporter, "Money can't make man or woman. . . . It isn't who you are, nor what you have, but what you are that counts."

Margaret Tobin Brown was an energetic champion of human rights who spoke her mind throughout her entire life. She used her money and her fame to help those less fortunate than herself, and she was probably only half-joking when she said that separating rich people from their money to help the poor had been the joy of her life. The unsinkable Margaret Brown was without question a remarkable and unforgettable woman.

Margaret made every day of her life an adventure.

In Your Community

Margaret Tobin Brown spent her life helping other people. What can you do to share your talents with others? Can you rake leaves for a neighbor or return library books for a sick friend? Can you paint a picture for your grandparents or let your little sister play with one of your special toys? Think of ways you can share your good fortune with someone else.

Margaret Brown also loved traveling to see new places and meet new people. Talk to the other members of your family, and think of a way you can learn about new people and places.

Timeline

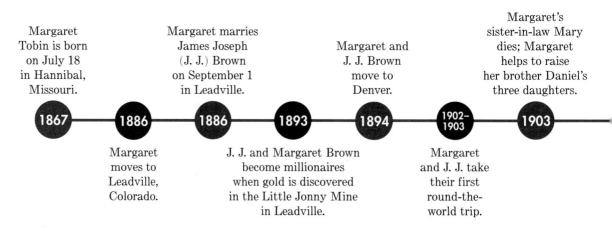

Margaret Tobin is born on July 18 in Hannibal, Missouri.
1867

Margaret moves to Leadville, Colorado.
1886

Margaret marries James Joseph (J. J.) Brown on September 1 in Leadville.
1886

J. J. and Margaret Brown become millionaires when gold is discovered in the Little Jonny Mine in Leadville.
1893

Margaret and J. J. Brown move to Denver.
1894

Margaret and J. J. take their first round-the-world trip.
1902–1903

Margaret's sister-in-law Mary dies; Margaret helps to raise her brother Daniel's three daughters.
1903

Visit a new park in your area, or take a bus ride to a nearby town. Plan a family vacation: get maps, read about the places you will visit, and learn about the sights you will see. When you go on

your trip, be sure to keep a scrapbook to help you remember all you have seen and done.

Margaret especially loved the culture and the language of France. Go to your library and ask the librarian for a book with easy French phrases. Can you learn to count to ten in French? See if you can find a tape or CD with simple French songs to sing along with!

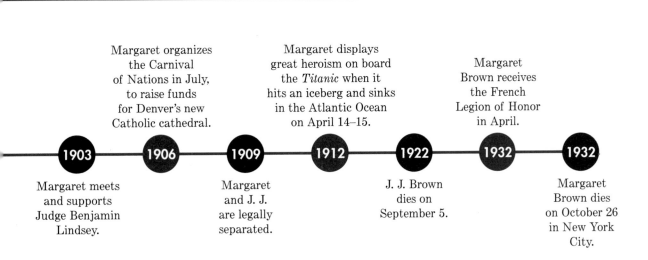

1903
Margaret meets and supports Judge Benjamin Lindsey.

Margaret organizes the Carnival of Nations in July, to raise funds for Denver's new Catholic cathedral.
1906

1909
Margaret and J. J. are legally separated.

Margaret displays great heroism on board the *Titanic* when it hits an iceberg and sinks in the Atlantic Ocean on April 14–15.
1912

1922
J. J. Brown dies on September 5.

Margaret Brown receives the French Legion of Honor in April.
1932

1932
Margaret Brown dies on October 26 in New York City.

To Find Out More

Here are some additional resources to help you learn about Margaret Tobin Brown, Colorado, and the Titanic disaster:

Books

Blos, Joan. *The Heroine of the Titanic.* Morrow Jr. Books, 1991.

Fradin, Dennis Brindell. *Colorado.* Children's Press, 1993.

Kent, Deborah. *The Titanic.* Children's Press, 1993.

Organizations and Online Sites

Molly Brown House Museum
1340 Pennsylvania Street
Denver, Colorado 80203
http://www.mollybrown.org
Learn more about Margaret's life, see pictures of her and her family, and tour her beautiful home in Denver.

Molly Brown Birthplace and Museum
P. O. Box 1548
Hannibal, MO 63401
http://www.mollybrown museum.com
Tour Margaret's childhood home in Missouri, and learn about Margaret and the history of Hannibal.

The Titanic Historical Society Inc.
P. O. Box 51053
Indian Orchard, MA 01151
http://www.titanic1.org
Explore this site's information on the Titanic and its passengers.

Index

About the Author

Charnan Simon lives in Madison, Wisconsin, with her husband and her two daughters. She is a former editor of *Cricket* magazine and has written many books for young people, including Community Builders biographies of Andrew Carnegie, Jane Addams, Jesse Jackson, and others. Ms. Simon would be happy to possess one-half of Margaret Tobin Brown's energy, good humor, and zest for life.